Pathfinder 19

A CILT series for language teac[h]

Drama in the languages classroom

by Judith Hamilton

and

Anne McLeod

C*i*LT

Other titles in the PATHFINDER series:

Acknowledgement

The photos in this book show pupils from Queensferry High School, South Queensferry, Scotland.

First published 1993
Copyright © 1993 Centre for Information on Language Teaching and Research
ISBN 1 874016 07 0

Cover by Logos Design and Advertising
Printed in Great Britain by Oakdale Printing Co Ltd

Published by Centre for Information on Language Teaching and Research, 20 Bedfordbury, Covent Garden, London WC2N 4LB.

Contents

Introduction

Language teachers have in recent years shown an increasing interest in the experiences of their colleagues in drama departments. This book intends to support, encourage and inform teachers of foreign languages who are already involved or who would like to get involved in this area. The authors have worked in the same department together with their colleague, the Principal Teacher of Drama, Sandra Reid, who helped them to develop their own skills and materials.

Drama has a great deal to offer language teachers. Both subjects want learners to be:

★ active participants;
★ willing communicators;
★ responsible;
★ flexible;
★ open-minded;

and to be able to:

★ develop and transfer the skills they acquire in one set of circumstances to another, different set of circumstances.

1.   Why should I do it?

Drama is about *making* real meanings

Much has been written about what is communicative or not in language teaching and perhaps no term is so widely misused as 'communication'. One of the critical factors for determining how communicative any language activity is, is to ask the question 'would it occur naturally in the mother tongue under these circumstances?'. Much of what we say in language classrooms is denuded of any real meaning and is only tolerable because we do **not** say it in the mother tongue.

How are we to offer our learners the scope for 'learning how to mean', to adopt a phrase of Michael Halliday's, while at the same time keeping the level of difficulty to one at which they can happily cope and feel encouraged? How can we use the target language to make real meanings **in** the language rather than to talk **about** the language? Drama offers us the context in which to do this.

Where drama techniques and language teaching meet

The use of drama techniques fits naturally into the theoretical context of recent studies into the nature of language and language learning. Language teachers have over the years been offered many theories which would supposedly enhance, or perhaps even transform their teaching. Some of these have turned out to be at best irrelevant distractions. Yet all teachers operate on the basis of 'theories' of one kind or another, consciously or unconsciously. They come from a variety of sources and are often referred to as 'beliefs'. When the findings/recommendations of researchers go against our 'beliefs', and especially when they nevertheless influence, as some of them do, national policy and hence our work in the classroom, the tendency is to reject 'theory' as a whole, especially since many teachers remember only too well the results of the implementation of some of the more bizarre of these. All the more reason therefore for us as practitioners to examine, analyse and evaluate our own teaching practice. All good teachers are action researchers in their classrooms.

One of the principal concerns at the moment is to find ways of creating for our pupils a more natural language learning environment. We know that the classroom is not the best place to get to grips with a foreign language. Given the chance we would opt for having our pupils live in the foreign language community and dispense with our services altogether. Because we know that two weeks living with a foreign family is probably worth a year of our teaching, we try as much as possible to recreate such an experience in our classroom with posters, realia and sounds that reflect this, increasingly using the target language ourselves, encouraging our pupils to say what they mean in the language and correcting for the most part only those errors that impede communication. We no longer simply **describe** the rules of the language; we are concerned with having our pupils **perform** in the language. Yet we know that this performance is not something wholly within our control, not something we can force from unwilling pupils. There has to be a reason, a context, the motivation or need to use the language. It is in the creation of such contexts for communication that drama techniques have such a strong claim on our attention.

The methodological continuum

We have attempted in this diagram to represent a rationale for those who are considering using drama techniques. It should be clear from this how drama techniques might play a useful role whatever a teacher's personal *point de départ*.

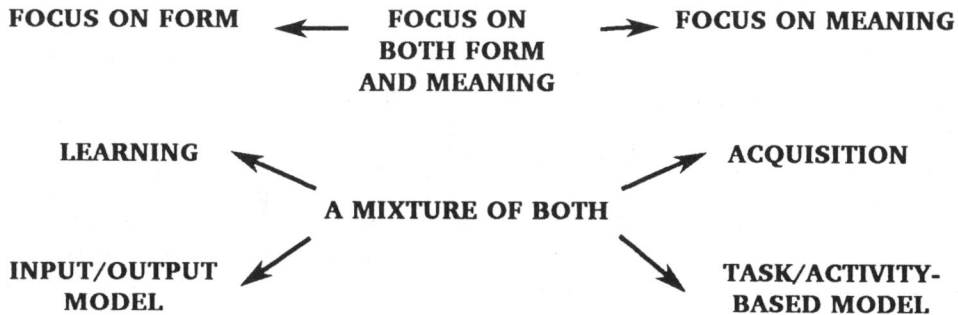

FOCUS ON FORM   ←   FOCUS ON BOTH FORM AND MEANING   →   FOCUS ON MEANING

LEARNING   ↖   ↗   ACQUISITION

A MIXTURE OF BOTH

INPUT/OUTPUT MODEL   ↙   ↘   TASK/ACTIVITY-BASED MODEL

I teach/present the structure, my pupils learn through imitation and practice.	*I like to create the need for my pupils to use a particular structure and at the same time encourage the building up of their own internalised grammar system.*	*My pupils are taught to be resourceful and to find within themselves, using a variety of sources and strategies, a way of meeting their linguistic needs.*

No matter what kind of teacher you are or whereabouts on the continuum you would place yourself, drama still has something to offer.

I am a traditional teacher

I believe in teaching structures and grammar. I want my students to practise 'mon/ma/mes', 'son/sa/ses'.

*I can use the **Circle memory game** (see p10) and focus on the following structures:*

***Student A**: J'ai perdu **mon** passeport.*
***Student B**: Elle a perdu **son** passeport. Moi, j'ai perdu **mes** clefs.*
***Student C**: Elle a perdu **son** passeport. Il a perdu **ses** clefs. Moi, j'ai perdu **ma** bague.*

I want the best of both worlds

*I have a structure in mind, but I believe that pupils can best learn this in a **meaningful situation** through a **meaningful activity**. For example:*

> *J'ai perdu ...*
> *Il/Elle a perdu ...*

*I can use the **Circle memory game**. I am not primarily interested in 'mon/ma/mes'. I am more interested in words which carry meaning (i.e. nouns and pronouns). The game creates the need for students to use the correct 'il/elle' pronoun. From the students' point of view, calling a girl 'il' is 'wrong' and they actually feel it, because the person referred to, as well as the rest of the class, will react to the mistake. The need to get this right is created by the **game** and not by me as teacher. The game gives students a meaningful context for saying 'J'ai perdu ...' etc.*

I am a 'humanistic' teacher

I believe in experiential learning and the development of the individual.

I want to create an atmosphere conducive to communication in which my pupils only ever use language where they actually 'mean' in the Halliday sense.

*My pupils acquire a given structure **because** it, or something very like it, comes up as we go along.*

*I would use the **Circle memory game** because it is a way of making students feel good about themselves - they really can recall a great deal. This way they learn to help each other. Whether I decide to do it with 'J'ai perdu ...' or with 'J'aime ...' or 'Je suis allé à ...' is neither here nor there. It's the experience of success and co-operation that counts.*

Drama encourages pupil talk

Given the importance of talk in our classrooms it is vital to create an atmosphere in which the learners are not afraid to open their mouths and speak in the target language. This kind of stress-free, fun teaching encourages pupils to participate without embarrassment since the emphasis on completing the task in hand distracts the learner from the language and focuses their attention firmly on this task - i.e. they stop worrying 'Help, she's going to ask me to say something in French' , because what they want to do is participate in the game/activity. Drama is a way of building confidence and often succeeds where other methods have failed.

It is hard to imagine anything else that offers to language teachers such a wide variety of types of talk, e.g. monologues, paired speaking, role-plays, group discussions, reporting, talking in response to other stimuli, problem-solving, developing scenarios, acting out, etc. From explaining, complaining, praising, disagreeing to exhorting, apologising and requesting - there is no language function that drama is not capable of easily encompassing.

Drama and the development of the individual

As methodology has changed over recent years towards more active production of the foreign language there has been a tendency for language teachers to regard learners as principally 'talking heads'. Drama on the other hand involves the whole person intellectually, physically and emotionally. It can lead, through the exploration of unknown or familiar situations, to insights about the self as well as other people, situations and places. Involving relations with others, it promotes social and adaptive skills which in their turn feed into the process of learning a foreign language. It allows for dealing with sensitive issues such as gender, race and conflicts in a sensitive and non-threatening way. Learners are encouraged to explore themselves and their reactions in relation to the outside world in a way which can be both strengthening and enriching.

Use across the ability range

The experiences offered in drama lend themselves very much to use with different year groups and to differentiation within the classroom. The activities can be as demanding or undemanding linguistically as the teacher chooses and the atmosphere should always be a non-threatening one in which all learners feel able to contribute something.

Once teachers have mastered a few essential techniques they are able to adapt them for use with learners of different levels of ability. For example, the *Circle memory game* (see p10) can easily be used to practice structures at different levels, as can the Paul Jones *Double circle* (p14), the *Find a partner technique* (p24) and many others. Drama activities can offer just as much to 5th year classes as to 1st year classes in terms of providing a context for language acquisition and a reason to use the target language in a meaningful way.

Lower ability learners have also much to gain from taking part in drama activities. Many of the activities described under 'Movement' (see p19) and 'Mime' (see p21) require the students to listen to the target language and respond in some way other than in speech. Many less able students find the production of language very difficult and can feel scared or even intimidated when asked to speak in front of their more able peers. Participation in 'Movement and Mime' activities integrates these students with the rest of the class and allows them to join in without feeling embarrassed or scared of not being able to perform. They derive great pleasure and pride from the knowledge that their contribution in such 'listen and do' activities is just as valuable as that of the others in the class, and a feeling of success when they realise just how much they can understand.

Exposure to such activities, whilst certainly beneficial in terms of language acquisition and development of listening skills, also leads to a building of confidence and to the student feeling less inhibited about actually trying to speak in the target language. Above all, drama allows the less-able student to achieve something worthwhile in the language classroom, and to actually enjoy it!

Drama in the National Curriculum

The National Curriculum Programmes of Study for Key Stages 3 and 4 make several specific as well as some oblique references to drama activities. It is clear that with such a heavy emphasis on **performance** in the language, teachers will need to pay attention to the psychological aspects of language learning in order to help their pupils perform in the tasks described. The examples below are taken from *Modern foreign languages for ages 11 to 16* (October 1990).

With regard to movement and gesture, pupils should be able to:

AT1/1a *'respond physically to individual words and phrases (e.g. one to four words), songs, poems, rhymes, with teacher support.'*

This suggests techniques such as are described in some detail in sections 6 and 7 of Chapter 3 of this book under 'Movement' and 'Mime'. These techniques would also fit in well with requirements such as in:

AT1/4c *'use non-verbal clues to aid understanding, where appropriate, e.g. use the clues from gesture, intonation, etc to solve problems.'*

or indeed in:

AT3/2a *'understand short phrases composed of familiar language and presented in context.'*

and:

AT3/2b *'respond to the above physically and orally.'*

6

Language games will become a more common feature of the classroom, not simply as recreation but as ways of helping pupils learn the language, e.g. :

> **AT2/1d**
>
> 'take part in activities conducted in the foreign language, e.g. answer questions, **join in games, perform role-plays.**'

Since much is made of talking in the foreign language, teachers will want to give consideration to the **creation of an atmosphere** within which their pupils can give of their best, and which is conducive to communication. Pupils are asked to:

> **AT2/10c**
>
> 'talk **freely** or with notes with variation in vocabulary, structure and tense ... in **discussion** about factual or **imaginative** material, e.g. can **role-play** reporting an accident from a photograph/picture series or video responding to questions of fact and opinion posed by others.'

or in:

> **AT2/4b**
>
> 'deliver short memorised or prompted talking ... on familiar topics.'

and in:

> **AT4/5a**
>
> '... compose or adapt simple dialogue for performance.'

Such activities demand a high level of pupil confidence as well as linguistic competence and this confidence will have to be created.

While in Key Stage 3 reference is made to gaining and holding 'the attention of their audience,' taking part in 'language games and improvised drama' as well as 'simulations of partly unpredictable situations', Key Stage 4 specifically mentions that 'learners should ... have ... frequent opportunities to: improvise on the basis of an agreed scenario; take on more extended roles in drama work'.

Mention of simulations and improvisations makes it quite clear that drama has a strong role to play in the National Curriculum in our subject. This book aims to provide teachers with a starting point in drama techniques.

7

2.   Can I do it?

Some popular misconceptions

Drama means:
- ★ kids hanging from the lights;
- ★ noise and chaos;
- ★ lots of sketches;
- ★ horrendous discipline problems;
- ★ you have to write a thousand role-play cards;
- ★ you have to have a talent for mime;
- ★ no written work;
- ★ embarrassing activities to do with touching people;
- ★ you need small practical set classes;
- ★ more action than talk;
- ★ an unacceptable amount of errors;
- ★ kids moving about all over the place;
- ★ you can't do it in the average classroom;
- ★ it's only a special type of teacher who can cope.

On the contrary

Using drama techniques can mean:
- ★ learners doing a fair amount of silent reading;
- ★ periods of quiet reflection;
- ★ an atmosphere of concentration;
- ★ learners co-operating to encourage good behaviour;
- ★ an absence of discipline problems caused by bored, unmotivated learners;
- ★ the blossoming of a previously silent and unco-operative pupil;
- ★ learners working at their desks in their own classroom;
- ★ the whole class listening to the teacher;
- ★ the whole class silently watching a group perform;
- ★ more work covered than the teacher ever deemed possible;
- ★ learners using the target language willingly and without inhibition.

You don't have to be an energetic, extrovert person to use drama techniques successfully in your classroom. Drama techniques can be successfully used by anyone, regardless of personality. Remember that drama is a **way of thinking** about teaching and learning. The trick is to stop thinking of yourself as a teacher of languages and to start thinking of yourself as a teacher of something **through** languages - a teacher of people, not a teacher of nouns, verbs, etc.

3. Essential techniques - all ages and levels

Once you have mastered a few basic techniques you will find yourself able to use them in a whole variety of ways with a whole variety of structures.

THE CIRCLE WHERE EVERYONE REMAINS SEATED

▷ Memory games

(Otherwise known as *I went to the market and I bought...* or *In my grandmother's suitcase...*)

Basic technique
One student says what they bought. Next student repeats first student's item and adds one of their own. All students listen carefully, as they will have to remember all the preceding items before adding their own. There must be no repetition of a previously mentioned item.

Varieties

★ *With real objects*
Fill a carrier bag with items most of which the students know already in the target language (e.g. classroom objects) or for which the word in the TL is identical or similar to English (e.g. *orange, banane, lion*). Student A removes an object and names it in the TL, student B takes an object, names the previous object and the one he or she has taken, and so on.

Using real objects lends interest to practising a whole variety of structures from *J'ai acheté, Je voudrais* to *J'aurais dû acheter* and *Ich hätte ... nicht vergessen sollen* (plus accusative!).

★ *Practising structures at different levels*

Beginners	Student A:	*J'adore Tom Cruise.*
	Student B:	*Elle adore Tom Cruise. Moi, j'adore le foot* etc.
Intermediate	Student A:	*Le weekend, je suis allé au cinéma.*
	Student B:	*Le weekend, il est allé au cinéma, et moi, j'ai regardé la télé* etc.
Advanced	Student A:	*Ich habe Angst, wenn ich allein bin.*
	Student B:	*Er hat Angst, wenn er allein ist, und ich habe Angst vor Spinnen* etc.

▷ Circular conversations

Student A:	*Bonjour. Comment ça va?*
Student B:	*Très bien, merci. Et toi?*
Student C:	*Moi, ça ne va pas.*
Student D:	*Tu as un problème?*
Student E:	*Oui. J'ai oublié mes devoirs.*
Student F:	*Quels devoirs?* etc

This can clearly be done at any level. Once learners have got the idea, they become very adept at it.

▷ Circular stories

Another variety is to use this technique to tell a story. This can be started by using a prompt card, by the teacher, or by an inventive learner.

▷ Pass the parcel

Just like the party game, but using different sized envelopes. The music stops. The student opens the large envelope. Stuck on the envelope inside is one of the following:

★ a number to be read aloud
★ a picture of a sport/activity/animal/musical instrument etc to be mimed for the rest of the class to guess in the TL
★ an instruction in the TL for a student to carry out
★ any ideas of your own!

Students carry out the task. Music starts again. When it stops, next student opens envelope etc.

THE CIRCLE WHERE PEOPLE MOVE IN ORDER TO FIND A SEAT

Do you like your neighbour?

Student A stands in the middle of the circle. Other students are all seated. The object of the activity is to find a seat. Student A asks a question of any student in the circle. The question should require a yes/no answer. For example: *Tu aimes ton voisin? Magst du Eis?* If the student's reply is 'yes', then everyone remains seated and student A continues to ask the question of other students. If the reply is 'no', then every student in the circle must change their seat as quickly as possible. In their new seat they must not be sitting beside either of their previous 'neighbours'. Student A must also try and find a seat. There will be one person left without a chair. This person continues to ask questions as before, and the same procedure is followed for changing seats. Speed is an important factor in the success of this activity.

This activity is useful as a warm-up to more complicated tasks, or in its own right as a means of practising questions. The same question, chosen by the teacher, may be asked by every student, or the activity can be made more open-ended by allowing the students to choose their own questions.

Movement by numbers

Basic technique
Teacher allocates the numbers 1-4/5 to individual students all round the circle, so that there are several 1's, 2's, 3's, etc. He or she calls out a number and the students who have been given this number stand up and change seats as quickly as possible. The teacher must also try to find a seat. One person will be left in the middle, and must call out another number between 1 and 4/5, and the same procedure is followed for changing and finding seats. Speed is essential (but safety is also important!)

Varieties
★ Instead of numbers, the teacher allocates other items such as letters of the alphabet, pets, sports, colours, etc.

★ In this variety it is possible for everyone to change seats at once. For example *Fruit salad*:

Teacher allocates the names of 4-6 fruits to students in the circle. Students change seats when their fruit is called. In addition, when *Fruit salad* is called out, **all** students must stand up and change seats.

Other ideas

Teacher allocates animals, all change on 'zoo'; teacher allocates facial features, all change on 'face'; teacher allocates colours, all change on 'rainbow' etc.

★ A further variation would be to hand out pictures of the items to the students. Once everyone has changed seats, students should pass their card to the person on their right before the next item is called out. This tests students' knowledge of various vocabulary items in the course of the activity.

★ Movement with mime. As above, but pupils must mime as they move, e.g. playing tennis, kicking a football, etc. You can also do this with the adjectives of mood: *terrifié, fatigué*, etc. On the call *Crise de nerfs*, all students move, miming their mood as they go.

▶ Banana, banana, banana

Basic technique
Every student is given the name of a different fruit or vegetable. The teacher stands in the centre of the circle and calls out the name of one fruit/vegetable three times, as quickly as possible. The student who has been given the name of this fruit/vegetable must shout it out once, before the teacher has called it out three times. If the student succeeds, she keeps her seat. If not, she must give up her seat to the person in the middle.

Varieties
★ Other vocabulary areas may be chosen e.g. sport and hobbies, school subjects, household objects, classroom objects, animals, Christmas presents, clothes, etc.

★ Students are given a card with a picture of the item. (Each student must be given a different card). Proceed as above, but now and again the teacher asks students to pass the card to the person on their right/left.

THE DOUBLE CIRCLE (PAUL JONES)

Basic technique
You need:
    ★ Inner circle facing out
    ★ Outer circle facing in - same number in each so each student has a partner (see photo)
    (Students may be seated or standing)

You give a task to the whole group. They carry this out. You then tell one circle (e.g. the outer one) to move to their left or right. Thus each person has a new partner. You repeat the task (or give another task). The changing of partners continues until the end of the exercise. This offers an endless variety of opportunities for speaking at all levels. Some are listed below.

You can:

★ practise basic structures
  - ask your partner where she lives
  - ask your partner what he got for Christmas
  - talk to your partner about how you both spent the weekend
  - talk about what you would each do if you had £1,000

★ cover a variety of topics - talk about
  - the weather
  - your likes/dislikes at school
  - your pets
  - yesterday's TV programmes
  - your favourite food etc

★ or at a higher level
  - feminism
  - the death penalty
  - environmental pollution
  - how to improve conditions for pupils in your year group

★ include movement
  - put your hand on your partner's head and wish her/him Merry Christmas
  - stand back to back and talk about the weather

★ use it for mime on its own
  - you are playing tennis
  - you are playing a duet on the piano

★ use it for mime and talk
  - you are setting the table - discuss what's for tea

- you are eating spaghetti - talk about your holiday in Italy

★ use it with cue cards
- lost property - a selection of pictures of lost object, time and place lost on the card (sufficient to have one card per pair). Pupils are in the Lost Property Office and must build a conversation round the pictures (see illustration).
holidays - pictures of hotel, weather, means of transport

Cue cards: lost property

THE CHAIN

Basic technique
One large circle but students start in pairs facing their partners.

This is similar to the Paul Jones but leads to a tighter circle which can be less inhibiting and is good as a warm-up.

The teacher chooses a structure which students will use throughout the activity. This should initially be very simple - e.g. Student A: *Bonjour, ça va?* Student B: *Ça va bien, merci.*

However, they have to say this to each other while carrying out another instruction:

e.g.　　Greet your partner and jump up and down five times.

The students facing in one direction now move on to their next partner as in the 'chain' in the eightsome reel. A further instruction is given:

e.g.　　Greet your partner and put both hands on your head.

The movements to be carried out can become increasingly complex: 'Put your right hand on your partner's left shoulder and your left hand on her/his knee/foot and greet her/him'.

It is fun to get partners to stand back to back and call their 'conversation' over their heads to each other at the end.

BEATING TIME TECHNIQUES

Basic technique
This activity is best done seated in a circle. The teacher sets up a rhythm by, for example, tapping her knees twice then snapping her fingers once, pausing, before continuing the rhythm, to allow for something to be said in the gap. Pupils speak in turn around the circle, without repeating what anyone else has already said.

Varieties
★ Pupils say anything at all in the target language

★ A topic is chosen (e.g. animals, food, sports, etc) and pupils must name in the target language items which come under this heading

★ Numbers - straight counting

★ Numbers - counting backwards

★ Counting up in odd/even numbers

★ Counting up in 5's, 4's, etc

★ Alphabet forwards and backwards

★ Each new word must begin with the last letter of the previous word (e.g. *lait*, *thé*, etc).

★ Word association - Teacher gives a word (e.g. school). Each student in turn must give a word in the target language which he associates with the school (e.g. homework, teacher, etc).

★ Word association - Teacher gives a word (e.g. school). A student gives a word which he associates with this (e.g. pencil). Next student gives a word he associates with the previous word (e.g. wood), and so on.

If a student fails to say anything when it is his turn, or repeats an item that someone else has already said, he should stand up, and at the end of the 'round' be given a forfeit (e.g. dance the Highland Fling, do the Twist in slow motion, etc.)

Follow up
This activity can also be made into a memory game. Students must try to remember what other students said. Teacher can then point to a particular student and ask the rest of the group what he said, or teacher can ask one student to go round the circle trying to remember what each of the other students said.

Tip
The teacher should lead the time-beating and students should be asked to follow his/her lead and beat in time with the teacher. If not, the beat gets faster and faster and there is not enough time for each student to speak.

MOVEMENT

We are starting with movement because it is easier than mime! If you have never asked your students to move out from behind their desks, do not assume that they will be able to move around safely or sensibly! Students must be taught how to move around the classroom in an acceptable manner (or the maths department downstairs will complain!)

'Bring me something...'

Students are divided into teams. Teacher calls out 'Bring me something red/round/made of wood/etc'. The first team to produce a suitable item wins the point.

'Bring me something you could use to ...'

Teacher calls out as before, e.g. 'something you could use to stir your tea'. Each team must find a suitable object and mime the activity (e.g. stirring tea with a pencil).

Commands

This can be done whole class, in teams, in named groups

e.g.
★ Blue group, put your hands on your heads
★ Green group, pick up the telephone
★ Team A, sit on the floor
★ Team B, form a circle, etc

▶ Simon says

▶ 'Do this if ...'

e.g.
- ★ Stand up if you like cheese.
- ★ Stand up and jump up and down if you have long hair
- ★ Stand up on one leg if you saw *Eastenders* last night
- ★ Pull your right ear if you want to go home
- ★ Change seats if your surname begins with B, etc.

▶ Moving furniture

Teacher issues instructions

e.g.
- ★ Make your area of the classroom into a train compartment
- ★ Make your area of the classroom into a room in a house
- ★ Make your area of the classroom into a restaurant
- ★ Make your area of the classroom into a pet shop
- ★ Make your area of the classroom into a hospital ward, etc.

An extension of this activity would be to have a suitable conversation in the space created.

▶ Team game

One member of each team stands at the front of the classroom facing the board and blindfolded. The teacher points to one seated person in the opposing team. On the word 'Go' they try to reach the board before the blindfolded person points in their direction. If they reach the board, the now blindfolded person gives them a task.

▶ The birthday line

Students are asked to make one long line starting with the people whose birthdays fall in January and ending with those whose birthdays are in December. Once they are in the correct place for the months, they sort themselves out in order of the date of the month as well. This can lead on to other words on the birthday theme or indeed into horoscopes, where the dividing line is not the calendar month but the horoscope group.

MIME

This may seem a daunting area for a non-drama specialist, but you can build up from simple, warm-up mime activities to activities which demand good co-ordination and observation on the part of the learners. If your school has a drama specialist, get help - it makes all the difference.

Don't assume that a mime activity means no foreign language production from the students. While mime is an excellent vehicle for 'listen and do' activities, students can also be asked to respond orally to mimes done by others in the class, as in 'miming and guessing' games.

Listen/read and mime

Numbers
Individual students are asked to form the shape of a number (1-9) with their body, or pairs of students are asked to form the shape of two-digit numbers. (This can either be a 'listen and do' activity, where the teacher calls out a number in the target language for the students to mime, or it can be a guessing game, where students choose their own numbers to be guessed by the rest of the class in the target language).

Alphabet
As above, but forming letters of the alphabet. Groups of students can be asked to form whole words.

Shapes and sizes
As above, but students individually, in pairs, or in groups must form shapes and sizes as indicated by the teacher in the TL, e.g. *Formez un petit circle*; *Formez un grand carré*, etc.

Sports
Again this can be 'listen and do' or a guessing game. The teacher can call out sports for pupils to mime, or pupils can mime sports for others to guess.

Slow motion
A variation on the above. Students do their mimes in slow motion (*in Zeitlupe, au ralenti*). This requires better co-ordination and more concentration in order to mime as slowly as possible. It need not be restricted to sports. Students could for example be asked to dance a tango, or do the twist in slow motion. This activity is an excellent warm-up.

Musical instruments
The teacher calls out a musical instrument and students play that instrument. Alternatively, groups of students can form the shape of the instrument, and one student is asked to 'play' it. Eventually an orchestra/rock group/band of different instruments can be formed on the teacher's instructions. One pupil acts as 'conductor'. A melody is chosen and performed by the class, who mime and also sing in the manner of their instrument.

Walking on ...
The teacher tells the pupils to imagine that they are walking on different surfaces, e.g. ice, hot stones, mud, stingy insects, etc.

Miming to a story
You can devise your own stories, but here are some ideas:

★ crowded airport terminal - bomb scare
★ six people in a lift which gets stuck

★ people in a bank which is held up by robbers
★ disco: fire alarm goes off

Port and starboard

This is a well-known Brownie/Guides game. The following are the target language terms we use:

port	bâbord	Backbord
starboard	tribord	Steuerbord
land in sight	terre en vue	Land in Sicht
all hands on deck	tout le monde sur le pont	Alle Mann auf Deck
raise periscope	sortez le périscope	Periskop 'rauf
captain's coming	voilà le capitaine	Der Kapitän kommt
man overboard	un homme à la mer	Mann über Bord
the chef's gone	le chef s'en va	Der Koch ist weg
the ship's sinking	le navire coule	Das Schiff sinkt
here's the chef	le chef arrive	Hier kommt der Koch
ship ahoy	navire en vue	Schiff ahoi

Ideas for group mimes (good for 'read and do' as well as extended 'listen and do')

★ Smugglers shifting goods
★ Members of a secret society moving crates of high explosives
★ Refugees loading possessions onto a cart
★ Removing a grand piano down a narrow stair
★ Toys in toyshop start to move at midnight
★ An ambush
★ Setting up camp
★ Astronauts assemble a space platform (slow motion)
★ Divers clearing wreck under the sea
★ Thieves in the night, etc

Miming and guessing

Using objects - 100 uses for a ...

Teacher passes an object round the class. Each student in turn must think of a use for it and mime accordingly. The other students must guess in the target language what the object is supposed to be or what the student is using it for.

In the manner of ...

Teacher prepares a list of adverbs on card. One student picks a card and must mime/carry out an activity chosen by the rest of the class in the manner of the adverb, e.g. open the door **furiously**, sing a song **passionately**, etc. The class must guess what the adverb is.

Statues/freeze frame

Groups of students think of a particular incident or scene, for example, a road accident, a rock concert, surgeons in an operating theatre, etc. They take up position and 'freeze'. Other students must guess what the scene represents.

One way of preparing this is to ask the students in their groups to think of a sentence or phrase which on its own indicates an entire situation, e.g. 'tickets, please', 'pass me the scalpel', and then to form the freeze frame.

Lost voice

Teacher prepares cards outlining a situation where things have gone wrong, e.g. your dog ate your homework, there's an elephant in the back garden, there's a snake in your bed, etc. One student picks a card and imagines that this has happened and that she has lost her voice. The student must mime in order to explain the situation to the rest of the class, who attempt to guess in the target language what is happening, until they arrive at the precise wording on the card.

FIND A PARTNER TECHNIQUE

This activity may be carried out either in a circle or in the normal classroom arrangement.

Basic technique

You need an even number of participants (Teacher may have to join in if there is an odd number of students). Teacher prepares pairs of cards, which are shuffled and then distributed, one card to each student. Students are not allowed to show their cards to anyone else. Teacher informs students of the task in the target language (e.g. find the person the same age as you, find the answer to your question, etc - see examples below). Students move around the room trying to find their partner. This must be done by speaking in the target language and not by looking at other students' cards.

Once students have found their partner, they may

★ return to their own seats. Cards may be gathered in and activity repeated.

★ sit down beside their partner and carry out a follow-up task (e.g. a conversation based on the topic on the cards).

★ report back to the teacher, who can sort out any mistakes or problems.

The teacher should circulate amongst the students while they are attempting to find their partners and help out as necessary.

Eventually only a few students will be left standing. If they cannot match up their cards then obviously a mistake must have been made. The teacher can then ask each pair to read out their cards, and check whether or not they have found the correct partner.

Varieties
Find your partner (ideas for cards)

Task:	Find someone with the same Christian name as you
On cards:	Christian name and surname (e.g. Marc Dupont, Marc Leclerc, etc)

Task:	Find someone with two digits in their phone number the same as yours
On cards:	Phone numbers (e.g. 44 64 22, 44 23 68, etc).

Task:	Find someone with the same pet as you
On cards:	Pictures of pets

Task:	Find the person who plays this sport/with the picture of this sport
On cards:	Pictures of sports and sentences (e.g. tennis racquet and *Je joue au tennis*)

Task: Find the person whose phrase, when combined with yours, makes sense

On cards: One half of a coherent dialogue (e.g. *Tu vas au cinéma demain?* and *Ah non, demain j'ai trop de devoirs*)

Task: Find the sentence whose phrase, when combined with yours, makes a sensible sentence

On cards: Half a sentence each (e.g. *Mon frère a beaucoup de problèmes avec son prof de maths ...* and *... parce qu'il ne fait jamais ses devoirs.*)

Task: Find a person who is free at the same time as you and fix a date

On cards: Time of a possible date (e.g. *Lundi soir à sept heures* and *Lundi soir à neuf heures*

Task: You are a spy. You have to find your fellow agent who has the same secret codeword as you. You have to drop this word or phrase into a normal conversation otherwise the enemy agents will pick it up as they have 'bugged' the room. (NB you can do this with a large class where the students have to meet up with two or more agents to form a cell or network of spies).

On cards: A secret codeword or phrase (e.g. *étranger*)

4.   Simulations, improvisations & creative role-play

There is a vast difference between role-play as envisaged by examination boards and many textbooks and the way in which drama teachers use these activities. Here we are looking at ways of engaging the imagination of the participants so that the language they use arises naturally out of the situation. The purpose behind the activities we are about to describe is therefore not to practise particular structures, vocabulary or topics. This is perhaps best illustrated by the following case study.

Case study

Class SIII (in England SIV) - 30 students of mixed ability

The students were asked in groups to think of a sentence or phrase that in itself summed up an entire situation. Someone chose *Passez-moi le scalpel!*, the latter word said hesitantly but with a French accent (we had taught our students to guess in this way rather than use English, and here, as so often, it was the correct word). The interaction with members of the class was as follows:

Teacher:	*C'est où?*
Student	*A l'hôpital*
Teacher	*C'est qui?*
Student	*Le docteur*
Teacher	*Plûtot chirurgien - et qu'est-ce qu'il fait?*
Student	*Une opération*
Teacher	*Qu'est-ce qui s'est passé?*
Student	*Il y a eu un accident!*

Other groups had similar fairly rapid exchanges to establish what they had chosen. From there all groups in the class made a freeze frame (see under 'Mime' page 24) to illustrate their chosen sentence. The group mentioned above illustrated an operating theatre with each member of the team of four working out exactly how to stand/lie, etc, in their chosen role.

Other class members speculated on the situation - *Victime* was hazarded correctly; *Infirmière* was given in response to a request *Comment dit-on 'nurse' en français?*.

The next step was to look back at how the victim had ended up on the operating table - *Il s'est fait écrasé?* from the teacher introduced a new construction which proved useful for a later expansion of the scenario.

The various groups moved back in time from their individual freeze frames. This group took as its starting point the moments just before the victim's arrival in hospital - general chit-chat between doctor and nurses, the bleeper announcing the arrival of the patient, preparation for the operation, etc.

This concluded that particular period and homework consisted of checking out any expressions they might need in order to develop their scene. Subsequent lessons developed the scenario involving members of another group being co-opted to play the role of policeman at the accident scene, victim's family, etc. The whole drama and many of the scenarios which had arisen in other groups then became the meat of an improvised news bulletin which was 'run' in the course of a normal period, involving interviews, reports, etc, all filmed on camcorder. Not the tidiest of lesson plans - indeed there was no lesson plan, since the whole thing had its own dynamic which was under the control of the students themselves. But no-one was idle or bored and all of them were operating in French throughout.

★ ★ ★

Let's now look at a **creative role-play arising from a stimulus** - you can use almost anything, e.g. concrete objects, a picture, sound effects, etc. These can spark off phone calls, paired role-plays, group improvisations, storytelling, mime, acting out, etc.

Remember that drama is **a way of thinking** about teaching and learning!

Case study

Class SV (in England lower VI) - 20 students of good ability who have just read *Ein Anruf von Sebastian* which deals with relationships both within the family and between boy and girl.

The book ends on a decision by the girl to phone Sebastian some 18 months after they split up. As a result of changes she has made both in her life and her personality, Sabine now feels able to take the initiative and re-establish contact (The details are in a sense immaterial - all books that we use now at this level deal with similar topics, if not exclusively, certainly contiguously).

Telephone calls make a good starting point to a whole lot of scenarios. In this case students worked in pairs improvising the conversation between Sabine and Sebastian, whose characters they had already studied in some depth. From this to their next meeting the pairs stayed in role. Each pair envisaged their own 'ending', happy or otherwise, which they subsequently wrote up as a final chapter of the book.

Inventing role-plays, improvisations and the like becomes relatively easy once language teachers abandon the notion of 'teaching the language' - i.e. vocabulary and structures of the language - as their only goal. Research into acquisition theory (Kraschen) and memory (Stevick) has been fundamental in our own reassessment of our teaching.

★ ★ ★

5.   How do I get started?

Some hints and tips

- Ask your drama colleagues for advice and help. Perhaps they might be able to team-teach with you?

- Ask your language colleagues/the FLA to take part in some co-operative teaching.

- Choose a class with which you already feel comfortable to start with. Remember that nothing succeeds like success! Once the pupils have enjoyed participating in one activity, they will be keen to try out another. Once you have had a first-hand experience of how much your pupils can get out of drama, you will be keen to try out other techniques and in particular try them out with other less motivated classes.

- Begin a normal lesson with a short 'warm-up' exercise (e.g.: 'Do you like your neighbour?' p13, 'Movement by numbers' p13, 'Beating time' p18, 'Mime' p21).

- Always stop an activity while the pupils are still enjoying it and asking for more.

- Teach your pupils to organise your classroom and how to move around in an acceptable manner (see under 'Movement' p20: 'Moving furniture').

Bibliography

Brandes D and H Phillips, *The gamesters handbook* (Stanley Thornes, 1990, vols 1 and 2)

Dixey J and M Rinvolucri, *Get up and do it!: sketch and mime for EFL* (Longman, 1978)

Halliday M, *Learning how to mean: explorations in the development of language* (Edward Arnold, 1975)

Hamilton J and S Reid, *In play* (Nelson, 1991)

Hodgson J, *The uses of drama* (Methuen, 1972)

Hodgson J and M Banham, *Drama in education* (Pitman, 3 vols: 1972, 1973, 1975)

Hodgson J and E Richards, *Improvisation* (Methuen, 1974)

Kraschen S D, *Principles and practice in second language acquisition* (Pergamon Press, 1992)

Maley A and A Duff, *Drama techniques in language learning* (Cambridge University Press, 1982, 2nd ed)

McGregor L, Tate M and K Robinson, *Learning through drama* (Heinemann Educational, 1977)

Moskowitz G, *Caring and sharing in the foreign language class* (Newbury House, 1978)

O'Neil C, *Drama guidelines* (Heinemann Educational, 1977)

Stevick E, *Teaching languages: a way and ways* (Rowley MA, Newbury House, 1980)

Wagner B J, *Dorothy Heathcote: drama as a learning medium* (Stanley Thornes, 1990)

Way B, *Development through drama* (Longman, 1967)